THE CROWN JEWEL

First published in 2019 by:

Fayda Books
Publishing & Distribution
2690 Campbellton Rd.
http://www.faydabooks.com
orders@faydabooks.com

© Copyright Fayda Books 2019
ISBN 978-0-9913813-9-5

No part of this book may be reproduced in any form without prior permission of the publishers. All rights reserved.

Cover Design Muhammadan Press
Typesetting: Etherea Design

Printed and bound in the United States

دُرَّةُ التَّاجِ

The Crown Jewel

The Crown Jewel and fundamental needs of the student (*murid*), regarding the essentials of the rules and requirements of the Tariqa Tijâniyya Sufi Path

A concise instructional handbook

by
ABDUL KAREEM BIN AL-ARABI

Translation by
SHAYKH HASSAN ALIOU CISSE &
SHAYKH ALHAJI LAWAL

2019 Edition edited by
HIBA AMATTULLAH

Thanks to Imam Cheikh Tidiane Cisse for the permission to translate, publish and print all works pertaining to Islam, Tariqa Tijaniyya and Fayda.

Those who believe, and whose hearts find satisfaction in the remembrance of Allah, for without a doubt in the remembrance of Allah do hearts find satisfaction

﴿الَّذِينَ آمَنُوا وَتَطْمَئِنُّ قُلُوبُهُم بِذِكْرِ اللَّهِ ۗ أَلَا بِذِكْرِ اللَّهِ تَطْمَئِنُّ الْقُلُوبُ﴾

Endowment

We wanted to republish this book that was originally written by our beloved Shaykh Hassan Cisse ☸, and make it available free, to anyone interested in learning about the Tijani Tariqa and its devotional prayers. A debt of gratitude will always be due to Shaykh Hassan.

This effort is brought to you through the financial contributions of some of the brethren. Their contributions should be considered as a Waqf (Endowment) that will earn them blessings for as long as the information benefits people.

These contributors in certain instances have asked that the reward be given to loved ones who have passed on. Therefore, this list of contributors is comprised of those that are still with us as well as those that have passed on. May Allah increase them. May this effort become an important source of Da'wa to the world. Amin

Khalifa Al-Hajj Abdullahi Niasse ☸, Khalifa Ahmed Dame Niasse ☸, Khalifa Shaykh Tijani Niasse, Shaykh Naziru Niasse ☸, Sayda Bilkhis ☸, Shaykh Saydi Aliou Cisse ☸, Shaykh Hassan Cisse ☸, Imam Cheikh Tidiane Cisse, Shaykh Mahy Cisse, Shaykh Omar Diop ☸, Teacher Muhammad Anan ☸, Maalam Idris Sufi ☸, Shaykh Jibril Madaha ☸, Imam Yusuf ☸, Al-Hajj Ahmed Dimson ☸, Hajja Halima Dimson, Ismail Dimson ☸, Imam Said Abdus-Salaam ☸, Hajja Salwa Abdus-Salaam

🕮, Shaykh TaHa Cisse 🕮, Al-Hajj Abdul Azim Mustafa 🕮, Shaykh Idris Baye 🕮, Shaykh Ahmed Tijani Favours 🕮, Brother Muhassan 🕮, Al-Hajji Sani Muhammad 🕮, Al-Hajj Kabiru Muhammad 🕮, Al-Hajj Jibril Otoo 🕮, Hajja Fatima Shinkafi for Imam Cheikh Tidiane Cisse, Hajja Ayisha Jeffries Cisse for Willie & Anita Lovett 🕮, Dr. Ruhul Haqq 🕮 & Rabiyah Ellard, Hajja Jeanette Nu'man, Hajja Akanke Rasheed, Ishaq Majeed & Family, Maryann Riggins Massey for Harry Walter Massey III, Unanimous for Hajja Ayisha Jeffries, Juma Salaam for Morlie Idris Alamy 🕮, Ahmad Karim, Marjorie Karim, Jamillah Karim, Hud Williams, Yahya Williams, Lut Williams, Zayn Williams, Maryam Abdulkarim for Muhammad Abdulkarim, Ayatullah Mukarram for Herman Johnson (father).

Wa'Salaam

Ibrahim Ahmed Dimson
PUBLISHER, FAYDA BOOKS

In the name of Allah the Compassionate, the Merciful. The Prayers and Blessing of Allah be upon the Holy Prophet. Praise be upon the One Who has bestowed on us His infinite bounties and prayers, and the blessing of Allah be upon the Opener and the leader of the most straight path.

The needy servant of Allah, Abdul Karim Ibn Arabbinis (May Allah forgive his sins and accept his work by His grace) The Crown Jewel and fundamental needs of the student (murid), regarding the essentials of the rules and requirements of the Tariqa Tijâniyya Sufi Path.

The Tijani path has been endowed with secrets of the Lord and the favors of experiential knowledge of the Most High. As a gift to the student (*murid*) and a reminder to those favored with wisdom, it contains nothing but the orthodox authority or the accepted practice received from the disciples. May Allah the Most High accept this as a righteous work and a walking path, and may Allah the Most High include all in the fold of the Great Shaykh (Ahmed al-Tijani) the Seal of the Saints.

Ameen, Ameen a thousand times Ameen!

The compiler has said,

> May Allah have mercy on the disciple (*murid*) of the Tijani path for he is a Muslim (male or female) who understands the approach to Allah by wor-

ship. No matter how young he is, as long as he has been initiated into the Tariqa by a qualified and authorized person (*Muqaddam*), who has been duly initiated, authentically by a spiritual chain which ends at Shaykh Ahmed al-Tijani.

The Tijani Awrad includes the glorification of Allah (Dhikr) and the obligatory dhikr.

- *Wird* done in the morning and evening
- *Wazifah* done once daily
- *Zikrul Jumu'ah* done on Friday one half hour before sunset

This oath is taken to perform these Awrad, with the intention of continuous practice until death. Some of the other conditions are as follows:

- Avoidance of visits to other Walis that are living or dead with the intention of seeking spiritual benefits from them. This rule does not pertain to the Prophet ﷺ, the companions of the Prophet ﷺ, and other Tijani brethren, or Shaykhs of the tariqa Tijâniyya. You may visit other Sheikhs for general Islamic knowledge only.

- The student should not practice any other Tariqa. He has been sufficiently provided to gain spiritual rewards by reciting twelve times the special prayer "*Jawharatul Kamal*" with its prescribed conditions. (Ablution with water, in a sitting position, with clean surroundings, and properly covered)

- It is essential for the student to love and honor all the Walis (whether he belongs to the Tijani tariqa or not) without entertaining desires for deriving spiritual benefits from them.

The duties or classified prayers are:
The *wird* consists of:

- *Astaghfirullah* (100 times)
- *Salaatul-Ala Nabiyya* (100 times) (With any prayer on the Prophet, but Salaatul Fatihi is most complete)
- *La illaha illalah* (100 times)

The *wird* is performed in the morning (After Fajr Salat) and evening (After Asr Salat)

The conditions for the *wird*:

- Intention or '*Niyat*' must be made at the opening of the *wird*
- Purification by ablution (*wudu*), Ghusl, Tayyamum; whichever the situation dictates. (Dhikr can be done at anytime so women who are menstruating can make *wird* if they desire to or they can leave it until they are purified.)
- The cleanliness of *khabath*, is the cleanliness of clothes, the body, and the place of worship.
- The covering of the *Awrat*, is to cover the necessary parts of the body as required by Islamic Law. (Except with a legitimate excuse)
- Avoidance of talking, unless it is a word or two, which might be necessary in a given situation like replying to the call of parents, husband, or Shaykh

If any of these conditions are violated without good reason, the *wird* is void/invalid, and must be repeated with repentance of 100 Astaghfirullah, and a genuine determination not to repeat the same offences.

The one who misses his *wird* deliberately must make it up. It is optional for the sick and the menstruating women or the women bleeding from childbirth to make up the *wird*. The *wird* is also invalid if you intentionally change the prescribed order (e.g. to start with *hailalah* instead of *Astaghfirullah*), or intentionally decrease or increase the *wird*. If any of these faults occur mistakenly then it can be rectified by reverting to the correct order whenever it is remembered during the *wird* and reading Astaghfirullah 100 times after completing the *wird*.

The Conditions for Achieving Excellence of the Wird (Optional)

- Consciousness and being conscientious

- To imagine being in the presence of the Holy Prophet ﷺ and the leaders (Shaykhs) and to maintain the thought, throughout the *wird* (if you are able).

- Face the Qiblah in the sitting posture of prayer (Jalsah). Recite Istiazah (Seeking refuge from shaitaan), then Bismillah Ar-Rahman Ar-Rahim and Al Fatiha. Read Qur'anic verses which concerns *Istighfar*, Salah Ala Nabi, and that which concerns *Hailalah*, each in its respective turn (according to the order of *wird*).

- Recite the '*Talbia*' before beginning the Istigfar of the *wird* "LABAIKA ALLAHUMA WASADIKA"

Things to avoid

- Reciting aloud
- Smiling
- Looking here and there
- Thinking of worldly things
- Reciting in a state of drowsiness

Forbidden Things

- Careless mistakes
- Reciting too fast, leading to omissions
- Laughing aloud

Permissible things

- Pointing or guiding another person with a hint
- Handing over something
- Reclining for rest without sleeping (Heavy sleep voids the *wird*, if the sleep is light then one can continue the *wird* from where he is sure he left off before dozing. One should then rectify the doubt by reading Astaghfirullah 100 times.

The best recommended time for the morning wird

The best time for the morning *wird* is after Fajr Salat, up to one hour and a half after the sunrise. Its imperative time extends until sunset, after which it's considered repayment.

It's also permissible to make *wird* before dawn, in the early morning ours of the night without an excuse, because of the high multitude of rewards for worshipping in the night. It can be started two hours after Isha salat and continue up until the Fajr prayer begins, if the prayer is in while still reciting, you must complete the *wird* and repeat it after Subh prayer.

The best recommended time for the evening wird

The evening *wird* begins after Asr prayer, and its imperative time extends up to dawn (Fajr). It can be made up if missed in the specified imperative time.

It is not permissible to recite the evening *wird* in advance in the daytime, even if there is an excuse.

It is permissible to recite the *wird* for the coming day in advance in the night, if you are expecting difficulties in making it during its prescribed time. But it must be recited in its proper order e.g., morning *wird* (if there are no expected difficulties or excuse you can also recite the *wird* at night in advance, because of the rewards of praying at night).

If the Iqamah for prayer is called you must stop the *wird* and perform the prayer. After the prayer, one must continue were you stopped (prayers always have first preference over *wird* and *wazifah*).

The wazifah consists of:

- Al-Fatiha (recited once)
- *Astaghfirul lahal 'Azimal Ladzi Laa Illahaa Illa Huwal Hayyal Qayyum* (30 times)
- *Salaatul Fatihi* (50 times)
- *La Illaha Illallah* (100 times)
- *Jawharatul Kamal* (12 times)

No alternative to Salatul Fatihi is acceptable, and if it's not recited then the *wazifah* is not valid. Therefore the *wazifah* is not compulsory until you know or are able to recite the Salatul Fatihi.

Those who are in transit and menstruating women may perform the *wazifah*, but must substitute twenty (20) Salatul Fatihi for the twelve (12) Jawharatul Kamal, Remember, the reciting of the Jawharatul Kamal requires both ablution with water and sitting in one place.

Rules for performance of wazifah

The rules governing *wazifah* are the same as the those governing the *wird*

- Should be recited in a clean environment
- You must have ablution
- Should be performed aloud in a ring of people seated (except for an acceptable excuse)
- The recitation should be in unison
- It is recommended to be done conscientiously, and like the *wird*, observe the order, and imagine the presence of the Holy Prophet ﷺ.
- The spreading of a clean white cloth in the center of the ring when reciting Jawharatul Kamal (We believe that the Holy Prophet ﷺ and the four Caliphs join the *wazifah* at this point)
- For reciting the Jawharatul Kamal, ablution with water is obligatory. Otherwise in case of Tayyamum, Jawharatul Kamal should be replaced with twenty (20) Salatul Fatihi
- *Wazifah* is permitted on the backs of animals or riding

in a vehicle on a journey, but the reciter must come down when he/she reaches the seventh (7th) Jawharatul Kamal, and sit down to complete the remaining five (5). Except in case of a lack of security or danger. In this instance the Jawharatul Kamal should be replaced with 20 Salatul Fatihi

- The late comer should join the group and proceed with them, and at the end he/she should recite the portion of what he/she has missed at the beginning up unti the place where he/she started with the group

- The stages are ended with the last three verses of Surah 37 Al-Saffat. (*Subhana Rabbika Rabbil 'izzati 'amma yasifun. Wa salamun 'alal-Mursalin. Wal hamdu lillahi Rabbil 'alameen*)

The practice in Fez (the first Zawiyah) is to recite the above mentioned item only at the end of Salatul Fatihi and Jawharatul Kamal. The Hailalah stage is ended with Sayyiduna Muhammadun Rasulullah Alaihi Salam-ullah.

- During the twelfth (12th) Jawaharatul Kamal, hands should be raised and opened (supplication) while reciting

- The conclusion of *wazifah* should be the recitation of Surah 33 Ayat 56 ("*Innallaha wa malaikatahu yusalluna 'alan nabi. Ya ayyuhalladzina amanu sallu 'alaihi wa salimu taslima…*")

- While the hands are still opened and raised, supplication and prayers should be offered secretly. After the prayers, wipe the face with the palm of your hands. Shake hands with the rest of the brothers/sisters in the circle, first from the right and then the left, and to whomever it's possible to shake with

- The Imam will take the responsibility for the errors that might have been committed during the *wazifah*
- The individual should rectify any potential errors by reciting 100 Astaghfirullah, as in the *wird*

Zikrul Jumu'ah on Friday evening

Hailalah/Zikrul Jumu'ah is strictly instructed to be performed after Asr prayer on Friday. In Fez their practice is to first perform the *wazifah* and then continu with the Zikr-Jummah (Haillalah) until sunset (without recording numbers).

The congregation of brothers and sisters is a necessary condition, if possible. It should be said loudly and in unison, while in a circle, otherwise it should be performed individually.

If business allows, the Zikr should begin one hour before the sunset

If done as an indidual, it is permitted to recite it atleast 1,000 times, or more At-tahlil (*La Ilaha Illallah*). The most is 1,600 times, which is the example of Shaykh Ahmed Tijani.

Strong emphasis is placed on obeying Allah's instruction and avoiding what is forbidden, and to observe the obligatory prayers in congregation whenever possible, behind the observer of the Prophet's 🕌 Sunnah and not behind the enemy of Shaykh Ahmed Tijani. The enemies of Shaykh Ahmed Tijani should be avoided even if it happens to be his own children

You should love all the companions of the Shaykh, and do good to them and be affectionate towards them, advise them wisely, and make every effort to practice other optional litanies (supplication) of Shaykh as often as possible.

You should recite Bismillah in the beginning of obligatory

prayers, aloud when the reading is aloud, and silent when the reading is silent. According to the practice of the Shaykh

The one who becomes fully conversant with the aforementioned principles may be qualified to be appointed Muqaddam (initiator), and should be of exemplary character.

He/She must fully appreciate the merits of following the Tariqa and must be knowledgeable of the rules of cleanliness, prayers, religion. He/She must be sensible, forgiving, trustworthy, zealous with doing good, generous, and not greedy. Otherwise, he/she should not be appointed as a Muqaddam. Rather, more importantly, that individual should be engaged in self purification. May Allah Most High protect us from fault and guide us to the good works and utterances. *Amin!*

Conditions Of Tijaniyyah Tariqa According To *Kitab Al-Fath Al-Rabbani* (The Godly Gnostic of what the followers of Tijanniyah would need)

There are forty (40) conditions, divided into two groups. The obligatory conditions and the conditions to obtain excellence. Further more, each one of the two parts is divided into another two parts… conditions related to the person and conditions relating to the prayers.

Conditions relating to the person

1. Receive permission from a pious Muqaddam with correct permission or authority

2. To observe the five obligatory salat in congregation if possible.

3. To recite Bismillahhir-Rahmanir-Rahim before the Fatihah

4. Taking your time in making Ruku and Sujud (if you

read Subhanna- Rabbiyal Adzeem slow then say it three times, if you read it fast say it six times)

5. To make Tahajud prayers at night
6. Keep making the Sunnahs before and after the Fard prayers
7. To be truthful
8. To be kind to your parents (Muslim or non-Muslim
9. To love Shaykh Ahmed Tijani (because of his love for Allah and he might help you become closer to Allah)
10. To have respect for the brotherhood of Tijaniyyah all over the world.
11. Don't cause harm to the brothers and sisters (The Brotherhood)
12. To respect the Walis (Friends of Allah)
13. Love all of Allah's creation, and act nicely towards them
14. The enemies of the Shaykh should also be your enemies.
15. To believe, surrender, and submit to all that is said by the Shaykh (as long as it is in the circle of Qur'an and Hadith). Remember, he will not come with a new revelation, but a deeper understanding
16. Not to criticize the Shaykh (Ahmed Tijani)
17. Don't take Allah's punishment and mercy for granted
18. Don't demonstrate being a Tijani. (Don't show off with the *wird*)

19. Don't neglect the *wird*
20. Do not give invitation into the Tariqah without permission. (Without being a Muqaddam in the Tijaniyyah)

The obligatory conditions relating to the persons

1. Avoid visiting non-Tijaniyyah Walis living or dead in order to seek spiritual benefits.
2. To abandon all other *wirds* except the Tijani's
3. To practice the *wird* until death

Essential conditions related to the *wird & wazifah*

1. One should be in a state of purification (wudu, tayammum or ghusl)
2. One's body, clothes, and place of worship should be clean
3. One should cover the necessary parts of the body, according to Islamic Law
4. One should avoid talking, unless absolutely necessary
5. One should make intentions at the beginning of the *wird*
6. In order to recite the Jawharatul Kamal, you must have ablution with water, be in a place where the capacity is for a minimum of six (6) persons to sit. (The Holy Prophet ﷺ, the four Caliphs, and yourself)
7. *Wazifah* should be done sitting down

Al-wird should be done in the morning after *Subh* (Fajr) and in the evening after *Asr*.

1. ASTAGHFIRULLAH

$$\text{اَسْتَغْفِرُ اللهِ}$$

(100 times)

2. ALLAHUMA SAULI ALA SAYYIDINA MUHAMMAD OR SALATUL FATIHI

اَللَّهُمَّ صَلِّ عَلَى سَيِّدِنَا مُحَمَّدٍ الفَاتِحِ لِمَا أُغْلِقَ وَالخَاتِمِ لِمَا سَبَقَ نَاصِرِ الحَقِّ بِالحَقِّ، وَالهَادِي إِلَى صِرَاطِكَ المُسْتَقِيمِ وَعَلَى آلِهِ حَقَّ قَدْرِهِ وَمِقْدَارِهِ العَظِيمِ

(100 times)

3. LA ILLA HA ILLALLAH

لَا إِلَهَ إِلَّا الله

(100 Times)

4. SAYYIDINA MUHAMMADUN RASULALLAH ALAIHI SALAAMULLAH

سَيِّدُنَا مُحَمَّدٌ رَسُولُ اللهِ عَلَيْهِ سَلَامُ اللهِ

(1 Time)

Al-wazifah should be done once in 24 hours.

1. BISMIL LAAHIR RAHMAANIR RAHEEM AL HAMDU LILLAHI RABBIL `AALAMEEN. ARAHMAANIR RAHEEM. MAALIKI YAWMID DEEN. EYYAAKA NA`BUDU, WA EYYAAKA NASTA`EEN. EH'DENAS SIRAATAL MUSTAQEEM.SIRAATAL LAZINA AN`AMTA `ALAYHIM; GHAYRIL MAGHDOOBI `ALAYHIM WALADDAALEEN.

    (1 Time)

2. ASTAGHFIRULLAH HAL AZEEM AL LADHI LA ILLA HA ILAH HUWAL HAYUL QAYUM

اَسْتَغْفِرُ اللهَ العَظِيمَ الَّذِي لَا إِلَهَ إِلَّا هُوَ الحَيُّ القَيُّومُ

    (30 Times)

3. ALLAHUMMA SALLI ALA SAYYIDINA MUHAMMADIL FATIHI LIMA UGLIQA, WAL-KHATIMI LIMA SABAQA, NASIRIL HAQQI BIL HAQQI WAL-HADI ILA SIRATIKAL MUSTAQIM,WA ALA ALIHI HAQQA QADRIHI WAMIQDARIHIL AZIM.

اَللَّهُمَّ صَلِّ عَلَى سَيِّدِنَا مُحَمَّدٍ الفَاتِحِ لِمَا أُغْلِقَ وَالخَاتِمِ لِمَا سَبَقَ نَاصِرِ الحَقِّ بِالحَقِّ، وَالهَادِي إِلَى صِرَاطِكَ المُسْتَقِيمِ وَعَلَى آلِهِ حَقَّ قَدْرِهِ وَمِقْدَارِهِ العَظِيمِ

    (50 Times)

4. SUBHANA RABBIKA RABBIL 'IZZATI 'AMMA YA-SIFUN. WA SALAMUN 'ALAL-MURSALIN. WAL HAMDU LILLAHI RABBIL 'ALAMEEN

سُبْحَانَ رَبِّكَ رَبِّ الْعِزَّةِ عَمَّا يَصِفُونَ وَسَلَامٌ عَلَى الْـمُرْسَلِينَ وَالْـحَمْدُ لِلّٰهِ رَبِّ الْعَالَمِينَ

(1 Time)

5. LA ILLA HA ILLALLAH

لَا إِلَهَ إِلَّا الله

(100 Times)

6. SAYYIDINA MUHAMMADUN RASULALLAH ALAIHI SALAAMULLAH

سَيِّدُنَا مُحَمَّدٌ رَسُولُ اللهِ عَلَيْهِ سَلَامُ الله

(1 Time)

7. ALLAHUMMA SALLI WA SALLIM `ALAA `AYNIR-RAHMATIR-RABBAANIYATI WAL YAAQUTATIL-MUTAHAQQIQATIL-HAAITATI BI-MARKAZIL-FUHOOMI WAL-MA`ANEE. WA NOORIL-AKWAANIL-MUTAKAWWINATIL-ADAMIYYI SAHIBIL HAQQIR-RABBANI AL BARQIL ASTA'I B IMUZUNIL ARBAHIL MALIATI

LI KULLI MUTA'ARRIDHIN MIN-AL BUHURI WAL-AWAANI. WA NURIKALLA MIL LADHEE MALA ATA BIHI KAWNAKAL-HAA'ITA BI-AM-KINATIL-MAKAANI.

8. ALLAHUMMA SALLI WA SALLIM 'ALAA 'AYNIL-HAQQIL LATI TATAJALLA MINHAA 'URUSHUL-HAQAAIQI 'AYNIL-MA'AARIFIL AQWAM SIRAATI KATTA MIL-ASQAM.

9. ALLAHUMMA SALLI WA SALLIM 'ALAA TAL'ATIL-HAQQI BIL HAQQIL-KANZIL A'ZHAM. IFADHATIKA MINKA ILAIKA IHAATATIN-NURIL-MUTALSAM. SALLALLAHU 'ALAIHI WA 'ALAA ALIHI SALATAN TU'ARRI-FUNAA BIHA IY YAH.

(12 Times)

10. INNALLAHA WA MALAIKATAHU YUSAL-LUNA 'ALAN NABI. YA AYYUHAL-LADZINA AMANU SALLU 'ALAIHI WA SALIMU TASLIMA. SALALLAHU ALAIHI WA ALA ALIHI WA-SAH-BIHI WA-SALAMA TASLIMA. SUBHANA RAB-BIKA RABBIL 'IZZATI 'AMMA YASIFUN. WA SALAMUN 'ALAL-MURSALIN. WAL HAMDU LILLAHI RABBIL 'ALAMEEN

اَللَّهُمَّ صَلِّ وَسَلِّمْ عَلَى عَيْنِ الرَّحْمَةِ الرَّبَّانِيَّةِ وَالْيَاقُوتَةِ الْمُتَحَقِّقَةِ الْحَائِطَةِ بِمَرْكَزِ الْفُهُومِ وَالْمَعَانِي، وَنُورِ

الْأَكْوَانِ الْمُتَكَوِّنَةِ الْآدَمِيِّ صَاحِبِ الْحَقِّ الرَّبَّانِي، ابْرَقِ الْأَسْتَعِ بِمَرْزُونِ الْأَرْبَاحِ الْمَائِلَةِ لِكُلِّ مُتَعَرِّضٍ مِنَ الْبُحُورِ وَالْأَوَانِي، وَنُورِكَ اللَّامِعِ الَّذِي مَلَأْتَ بِهِ كَوْنَكَ الْحَائِطَ بِأَمْكِنَةِ الْمَكَانِي،

اَللَّهُمَّ صَلِّ وَسَلِّمْ عَلَى عَيْنِ الْحَقِّ الَّتِي تَتَجَلَّى مِنْهَا عُرُوشُ الْحَقَائِقِ، عَيْنِ الْمَعَارِفِ الْأَقْوَمِ صِرَاطِكَ التَّامِّ الْأَسْقَمِ،

اَللَّهُمَّ صَلِّ وَسَلِّمْ عَلَى طَلْعَةِ الْحَقِّ بِالْحَقِّ الْكَنْزِ الْأَعْظَمِ، إِفَاضَتِكَ مِنْكَ إِلَيْكَ إِحَاطَةِ النُّورِ الْمُطَلْسَمِ، صَلَّى اللهُ عَلَيْهِ وَعَلَى آلِهِ، صَلَاةً تُعَرِّفُنَا بِهَا إِيَّاهُ

(1 Time)

Make dua after *wazifah*.

HASBUNA LAHU WA NI'MAL WAKEEL

حَسْبُنَا اللهُ وَنِعْمَ الْوَكِيلُ

450 Times

YA LATIF

يَا لَطِيفُ

129 Times

AL FATIHAH (1 Time)
SALATUL FATIHI (10 times)
SURAH IKHLAS (11 Times)

Translation of prayers/zikr

1. I ask Allah forgiveness of Allah the Great, who there is no God but He the Self-subsisting, Eternal.

2. Oh Allah bestow your blessing upon our Sayyid Muhammad.

3. There is no God but Allah

4. Our Master Muhammad the Rasulullah, may the peace of Allah be upon him.

5. In the name of Allah, Most Gracious, Most Merciful. All praises belong to Allah, Lord of the Worlds, Most Gracious. Most Merciful, Master of the Day of Judgment, You alone do we worship, and You alone do we seek for help. Show us the straight path, the path of those who have received your grace, not the path of those who have brought down wrath, nor of those who wander astray. Ameen!

6. I ask Allah forgiveness of Allah the Great, who there is no god but He the Self-subsisting, Eternal.

7. Oh Allah bless our Master Muhammad who opened what had been closed, and who is the seal of what

had gone before, he who makes the truth victorious by the truth, the guide to thy straight path, and bless his household as is the due of his immense position and grandeur.

8. Glory to thy Lord, the Lord of Honor and Power. He is free from what they ascribe to Him. (Surah 37, ayats 180, 131, 1820)

9. There is no god but Allah.

10. Our Master Muhammad the Rasulullah, may the peace of Allah be upon him.

11. O Allah, bestow Your benedictions and Your peace upon the source of the divine mercy and the veritable diamond that is enclosed in the citadel of every understanding and meaning and the light of the creatures becoming human beings, the owner of the lordly truth, the brightest flash of lightning going through the beneficial rain clouds that fills every water channels, vast oceans and smaller, and your shining light which fills the existence and encompasses every place.

12. Oh Allah, bestow your benedictions and your peace upon the source of the truth, from which the majestic realities manifest, the source of the perfect knowledge, your path perfectly straight.

13. Oh Allah, bestow Your benedictions and Your peace onto the manifestation of the truth with the truth, the supreme treasure, your showering of lights from you to you, the quintessence of the hidden lights. May Allah's infinite benedictions be showered upon him and his family with such special and most unique kind of benediction by which we are blessed to attain

knowledge of him.

14. 'Verily, Allah and His angels send blessings on the Prophet: O' you who believe! Send blessings on him, and salute him with a worthy salutation. Salutation be upon him and upon his Sahaba be peaceful salutation. Glory to thy Lord, the Lord of Honor and Power. He is free from what they ascribe to him.

Zikrul Jumu'ah

1. Hailalah/Zikrul Jumu'ah is strictly performed after Asr prayers on Friday. The congregation of brothers and sisters is a necessary condition, if possible. It should be said loudly in unison, in a circle, otherwise it should be performed individually.

2. If business allows, Zikr should begin one hour before the sunset.

3. If the individual cannot be with the congregation for a valid reason, he/she is permitted to recite 1,000 times LA ILA HA ILLALLAH, but no more than 1,600 times which is the example of Shaykh Tijani.

Hailalah should be done on every friday evening on Jumu'ah one hour before sunset:

1.	al-Fatihah	1 time
2.	Istighfar	3 times
3.	Salatul fatihi	3 times
4.	at-Tasbih	1 time
5.	at-Tahlil	1,000-1,600 times

6. at-Tadzil — 1 time
7. al-Fatihah — 1 time
8. Salatul fati — 3 times
9. Inna laha…. (Sura 33 ayat 56) — 1 time

www.ingramcontent.com/pod-product-compliance
Lightning Source LLC
Chambersburg PA
CBHW060345080526
44584CB00013B/922